CAPE EDITIONS 23

General Editor: NATHANIEL TARN

Selected Poems Georg Trakl

edited by Christopher Middleton
translated by
Robert Grenier, Michael Hamburger,
David Luke and Christopher Middleton

JONATHAN CAPE
THIRTY BEDFORD SQUARE
LONDON

This collection first published 1968
© 1968 by Robert Grenier, Michael Hamburger, David Luke
and Christopher Middleton
Translated from the German by Robert Grenier, Michael
Hamburger, David Luke and Christopher Middleton
Jonathan Cape Ltd, 30 Bedford Square, London, WC1

SBN Paperback 224 61510 6
      Hardback 224 61511 4

Some of the poems translated by Michael Hamburger, David
Luke and Christopher Middleton appeared in *Modern
German Poetry* (MacGibbon & Kee, 1962). The translators
and publishers are grateful for permission to reproduce
them here.

Printed and bound in Great Britain
by Richard Clay (The Chaucer Press), Ltd
Bungay, Suffolk

Contents

EDITOR'S NOTE

Georg Trakl was born on February 3rd, 1887, in Salzburg, Austria. His first mature poems date from the first half of 1910, his second year as a student of pharmacy in Vienna. Another crucial period was the winter of 1912–13, also in Vienna, during which he wrote 'Helian'. His year of military service (1910–11) was followed by restless wanderings between the cities of Salzburg, Vienna and Innsbruck. At one time, a friend complained that he was spending on wine quite enough to keep anybody else comfortably alive. Trakl's vices also included a number of narcotics and a haunting passion for his younger sister Grete, a brilliant pianist and hardly less eccentric a person than her brother. In July 1914, Ludwig Wittgenstein made over 20,000 crowns from his own patrimony to Trakl (Wittgenstein said of his poems: 'I do not understand them, but their tone delights me. It is the tone of a man of real genius'), but in August 1914 Trakl was drafted as a reserve lieutenant-pharmacist in the Austrian army, and less than three months later he took his own life in the military hospital at Cracow in Poland (November 3rd, 1914).

Trakl once called his inner life 'an infernal chaos of rhythms and images', and its tensions were of a kind seldom found outside characters in Dostoevsky. But these tensions are transfigured into the serial imagery and floating rhythms of his poems, and they become a vision of spiritual crisis in Europe: mysteries of death and love and regeneration enacting themselves as things fall apart and the centre cannot hold. His poems are part of that 'inner mystical construction' which his contemporary Franz Marc called 'the great problem of our generation'. The two poets with whom Trakl had the strongest kinship are Hölderlin and Rimbaud.

Otto Basil's monograph GEORG TRAKL (Hamburg, 1965) is the only full account of his life. Since 1947, a great deal has been written about his work: about a dozen books, twenty German and Austrian dissertations, and sixty articles.

C.M.

De Profundis

Es ist ein Stoppelfeld, in das ein schwarzer Regen fällt.
Es ist ein brauner Baum, der einsam dasteht.
Es ist ein Zischelwind, der leere Hütten umkreist –
Wie traurig dieser Abend.

Am Weiler vorbei
Sammelt die sanfte Waise noch spärliche Ähren ein.
Ihre Augen weiden rund und goldig in der Dämmerung
Und ihr Schoss harrt des himmlischen Bräutigams.

Bei der Heimkehr
Fanden die Hirten den süssen Leib
Verwest im Dornenbusch.

Ein Schatten bin ich ferne finsteren Dörfern.
Gottes Schweigen
Trank ich aus dem Brunnen des Hains.

Auf meine Stirne tritt kaltes Metall.
Spinnen suchen mein Herz.
Es ist ein Licht, das in meinem Mund erlöscht.

Nachts fand ich mich auf einer Heide,
Starrend von Unrat und Staub der Sterne.
Im Haselgebüsch
Klangen wieder kristallne Engel.

De Profundis

There is a stubble field on which a black rain falls.
There is a tree which, brown, stands lonely here.
There is a hissing wind which haunts deserted huts –
How sad this evening.

Past the village pond
The gentle orphan still gathers scanty ears of corn.
Golden and round her eyes are grazing in the dusk
And her lap awaits the heavenly bridegroom.

Returning home
Shepherds found the sweet body
Decayed in the bramble bush.

A shade I am remote from sombre hamlets.
The silence of God
I drank from the woodland well.

On my forehead cold metal forms.
Spiders look for my heart.
There is a light that fails in my mouth.

At night I found myself upon a heath,
Thick with garbage and the dust of stars.
In the hazel copse
Crystal angels have sounded once more.

[M.H.]

Menschheit

Menschheit vor Feuerschlünden aufgestellt,
Ein Trommelwirbel, dunkler Krieger Stirnen,
Schritte durch Blutnebel; schwarzes Eisen schellt;
Verzweiflung, Nacht in traurigen Gehirnen :
Hier Evas Schatten, Jagd und rotes Geld.
Gewölk, das Licht durchbricht, das Abendmahl.
Es wohnt in Brot und Wein ein sanftes Schweigen.
Und jene sind versammelt zwölf an Zahl.
Nachts schrein im Schlaf sie unter Ölbaumzweigen;
Sankt Thomas taucht die Hand ins Wundenmal.

Mankind

Round gorges deep with fire arrayed, mankind;
A roll of drums, dark brows of warriors marching;
Footsteps in fog of blood, black metals grind;
Despair, sad night of thought, despair high-arching;
Eve's shadow falls, halloo of hunt, red coin consigned.
Cloud, broken by light, the Supper's end;
This bread, this wine, have silence in their keeping.
Here do the Twelve assembled, numbered, stand;
They cry out under olive trees at night, half-sleeping.
Into the wound Saint Thomas dips his hand.

[C.M.]

Zu Abend Mein Herz

Am Abend hört man den Schrei der Fledermäuse,
Zwei Rappen springen auf der Wiese,
Der rote Ahorn rauscht.
Dem Wanderer erscheint die kleine Schenke am Weg.
Herrlich schmecken junger Wein und Nüsse,
Herrlich : betrunken zu taumeln in dämmernden
  Wald.
Durch schwarzes Geäst tönen schmerzliche Glocken,
Auf das Gesicht tropft Tau.

Towards Nightfall My Heart

At nightfall one hears the crying of bats,
Two black horses frisk in the meadow,
The red maple rustles.
To the wanderer the little wayside inn appears.
Glorious new wine and walnuts taste to him,
Glorious: to stagger drunk through the dusking
    wood.
In its black branches the grievous bells are pealing,
Dew-drops fall on his face.

[M.H.]

Rosenkranzlieder

AN DIE SCHWESTER

Wo du gehst wird Herbst und Abend,
Blaues Wild, das unter Bäumen tönt,
Einsamer Weiher am Abend.

Leise der Flug der Vögel tönt,
Die Schwermut über deinen Augenbogen.
Dein schmales Lächeln tönt.

Gott hat deine Lider verbogen.
Sterne suchen nachts, Karfreitagskind,
Deinen Stirnenbogen.

NÄHE DES TODES

O der Abend, der in die finsteren Dörfer der Kindheit
    geht.
Der Weiher unter den Weiden
Füllt sich mit den verpesteten Seufzern der Schwermut.

O der Wald, der leise die braunen Augen senkt,
Da aus des Einsamen knöchernen Händen
Der Purpur seiner verzückten Tage hinsinkt.

O die Nähe des Todes. Lass uns beten.
In dieser Nacht lösen auf lauen Kissen
Vergilbt von Weihrauch sich der Liebenden schmäch-
    tige Glieder.

Rosary Songs

TO MY SISTER

Where you walk, there it is autumn and evening,
A blue deer under trees and its music,
A lonely pond in the evening.

The flight of birds and its soft music,
Sadness settling over your eyes' curve.
Your slight smile and its music.

God has altered your eyelids' curve.
O Good Friday's child, at night stars seek
Your forehead's curve.

                                                [D.L.]

NEARNESS OF DEATH

O the evening deep in the sombre hamlets of child-
    hood.
The pond beneath the willows
Fills with the tainted sighs of sadness.

O the wood which softly lowers its brown eyes,
When from the solitary's bony hands
The purple of his enraptured days ebbs down.

O the nearness of death. Let us pray.
This night the delicate limbs of lovers
Yellowed with incense on warm pillows untwine.

                                                [M.H.]

Amen

Verwestes gleitend durch die morsche Stube;
Schatten an gelben Tapeten; in dunklen Spiegeln wölbt
Sich unserer Hände elfenbeinerne Traurigkeit.

Braune Perlen rinnen durch die erstorbenen Finger.
In der Stille
Tun sich eines Engels blaue Mohnaugen auf.

Blau ist auch der Abend;
Die Stunde unseres Absterbens, Azraels Schatten,
Der ein braunes Gärtchen verdunkelt.

Amen

Corruption gliding through the crumbled room;
Shadows on yellow hangings; in dark mirrors
The ivory sorrow of our hands is arched.

Brown beads trickle through fingers that have died
In the stillness
An angel's blue opium eyes unclose.

The evening also is blue;
The hour of our decease, the shadow of Azrael
Darkening a little brown garden.

[D.L.]

Trompeten

Unter verschnittenen Weiden, wo braune Kinder
   spielen
Und Blätter treiben, tönen Trompeten. Ein Kirchhofs-
   schauer.
Fahnen von Scharlach stürzen durch des Ahorns
   Trauer,
Reiter entlang an Roggenfeldern, leeren Mühlen.

Oder Hirten singen nachts und Hirsche treten
In den Kreis ihrer Feuer, des Hains uralte Trauer,
Tanzende heben sich von einer schwarzen Mauer;
Fahnen von Scharlach, Lachen, Wahnsinn, Trompeten.

Trumpets

Under trimmed willows, where tanned children play
And leaves blow, tone trumpets. A churchyard
  shudder.
Banners of scarlet crash through the maples' grief,
Riders along ryefields, empty mills.

Or shepherds sing at night and stags step
Into the circle of their fire, the grove's ancient sorrow,
Dancers fling themselves up from a black wall;
Banners of scarlet, laughter, insanity, trumpets.

[R.G.]

Die Ratten

Im Hof scheint weiss der herbstliche Mond.
Vom Dachrand fallen phantastische Schatten.
Ein Schweigen in leeren Fenstern wohnt;
Da tauchen leise herauf die Ratten

Und huschen pfeifend hier und dort
Und ein gräulicher Dunsthauch wittert
Ihnen nach aus dem Abort,
Den geisterhaft der Mondschein durchzittert.

Und sie keifen vor Gier wie toll
Und erfüllen Haus und Scheunen,
Die von Korn und Früchten voll.
Eisige Winde im Dunkel greinen.

The Rats

In the courtyard the autumn moon shines white.
From the roof's edge wild shadows drop.
A silence lives in empty windows,
Easily up into which leap the rats

And flit hissing here and there –
A greyish dust-haze reeks
After them from the latrine, through which
The spectral moonshine shivers.

And they scramble greedily, insanely
And overflow house and sheds
Full of grain, fruit.
In the dark icy winds whine.

[R.G.]

Helian

I

In den einsamen Stunden des Geistes
Ist es schön, in der Sonne zu gehn
An den gelben Mauern des Sommers hin.
Leise klingen die Schritte im Gras; doch immer schläft
Der Sohn des Pan im grauen Marmor.

Abends auf der Terrasse betranken wir uns mit
braunem Wein.
Rötlich glüht der Pfirsich im Laub;
Sanfte Sonate, frohes Lachen.

Schön ist die Stille der Nacht.
Auf dunklem Plan
Begegnen wir uns mit Hirten und weissen Sternen.

Wenn es Herbst geworden ist,
Zeigt sich nüchterne Klarheit im Hain.
Besänftigte wandeln wir an roten Mauern hin
Und die runden Augen folgen dem Flug der Vögel.
Am Abend sinkt das weisse Wasser in Graburnen.

In kahlen Zweigen feiert der Himmel.
In reinen Händen trägt der Landmann Brot und Wein
Und friedlich reifen die Früchte in sonniger Kammer.

O wie ernst ist das Antlitz der teueren Toten.
Doch die Seele erfreut gerechtes Anschaun.

Helian

I

In the lonely hours of the spirit,
Beautiful it is to walk in the sun,
Beside the yellow walls of the summer.
Softly the footfalls ring in the grass; but always
The son of Pan sleeps in the grey marble.

Evenings on the terrace we got drunk with brown
    wine.
Reddish the peach glows in the leaves;
Gentle sonata, happy laughing.

Beautiful is the quiet of the night.
On a dark plain
We meet with shepherds and white stars.

When autumn has come
Sober clearness enters the grove.
Calmed we wander beside red walls
And the round eyes follow the flight of birds.
At nightfall the white water sinks in funeral jars.

In bare branches heaven celebrates.
In pure hands the countryman carries bread and wine
And the fruits ripen peacefully in the sunny larder.

O how earnest is the countenance of the dear dead.
Yet a just regard delights the soul.

II

Gewaltig ist das Schweigen des verwüsteten Gartens
Da der junge Novize die Stirne mit braunem Laub
    bekränzt,
Sein Odem eisiges Gold trinkt.

Die Hände rühren das Alter bläulicher Wasser
Oder in kalter Nacht die weissen Wangen der
    Schwestern.

Leise und harmonisch ist ein Gang an freundlichen
    Zimmern hin,
Wo Einsamkeit ist und das Rauschen des Ahorns,
Wo vielleicht noch die Drossel singt.

Schön ist der Mensch und erscheinend im Dunkel,
Wenn er staunend Arme und Beine bewegt,
Und in purpurnen Höhlen stille die Augen rollen.

Zur Vesper verliert sich der Fremdling in schwarzer
    Novemberzerstörung,
Unter morschem Geäst, an Mauern voll Aussatz hin,
Wo vordem der heilige Bruder gegangen,
Versunken in das sanfte Saitenspiel seines Wahnsinns.

O wie einsam endet der Abendwind.
Ersterbend neigt sich das Haupt im Dunkel des
    Ölbaums.

II

Immense is the silence of the ravaged garden
When the young novice garlands his temples with
    brown leaves,
His breath drinks icy gold.

The hands stir the age of bluish waters
Or in cold night the white cheeks of the sisters.

Soft and harmonious is a walk past friendly rooms,
Where solitude is, and the rustling of the maple tree,
Where still perhaps the thrush is singing.

Beautiful is man and evident in the darkness,
When marvelling he moves his arms and legs
And silent in purple caves the eyes roll.

At vespers the stranger is lost in black November
    destruction,
Under rotted boughs, beside leprous walls
Where earlier the holy brother walked,
Sunk in the faint thrumming of his madness.

O how lonely the evening wind desists.
Fading, the head bows in the dark of the olive tree.

III

Erschütternd ist der Untergang des Geschlechts.
In dieser Stunde füllen sich die Augen des Schauenden
Mit dem Gold seiner Sterne.

Am Abend versinkt ein Glockenspiel, das nicht mehr
    tönt,
Verfallen die schwarzen Mauern am Platz,
Ruft der tote Soldat zum Gebet.

Ein bleicher Engel
Tritt der Sohn ins leere Haus seiner Väter.

Die Schwestern sind ferne zu weissen Greisen
    gegangen,
Nachts fand sie der Schläfer unter den Säulen im
    Hausflur,
Zurückgekehrt von traurigen Pilgerschaften.

O wie starrt von Kot und Würmern ihr Haar,
Da er darein mit silbernen Füssen steht,
Und jene verstorben aus kahlen Zimmern treten.

O ihr Psalmen in feurigen Mitternachtsregen,
Da die Knechte mit Nesseln die sanften Augen
    schlugen,
Die kindlichen Früchte des Holunders
Sich staunend neigen über ein leeres Grab.

Leise rollen vergilbte Monde
Über die Fieberlinnen des Jünglings,
Eh dem Schweigen des Winters folgt.

III

Overwhelming is the generation's decline,
At this hour the eyes of him who gazes
Fill with the gold of his stars.

At nightfall bells die that will chime no more,
The black walls on the square decay,
To prayer the dead soldier calls.

A pale angel
The son steps into the empty house of his fathers.

The sisters have gone far away to white old men,
At night the sleeper found them under the columns
    in the hall,
Returned from their sorrowful pilgrimages.

Oh how their hair curds with filth and worms
When he plants his silver feet therein,
And from bare rooms they move with dead steps.

O you psalms in fiery midnight rains,
When the servants with nettles thrashed the gentle
    eyes,
The childlike fruits of the elder tree
Marvelling stoop over an empty grave.

Softly yellowed moons roll
Over the fever sheets of the young man,
Before silence of winter comes.

IV

Ein erhabenes Schicksal sinnt den Kidron hinab,
Wo die Zeder, ein weiches Geschöpf,
Sich unter den blauen Brauen des Vaters entfaltet,
Über die Weide nachts ein Schäfer seine Herde führt.
Oder es sind Schreie im Schlaf,
Wenn ein eherner Engel im Hain den Menschen
    antritt,
Das Fleisch des Heiligen auf glühendem Rost
    hinschmilzt.

Um die Lehmhütten rankt purpurner Wein,
Tönende Bündel vergilbten Korns,
Das Summen der Bienen, der Flug des Kranichs.
Am Abend begegnen sich Auferstandene auf
    Felsenpfaden.

In schwarzen Wassern spiegeln sich Aussätzige;
Oder sie öffnen die kotbefleckten Gewänder
Weinend dem balsamischen Wind, der vom rosigen
    Hügel weht.

Schlanke Mägde tasten durch die Gassen der Nacht,
Ob sie den liebenden Hirten fänden.
Sonnabends tönt in den Hütten sanfter Gesang.

Lasset das Lied auch des Knaben gedenken,
Seines Wahnsinns, und weisser Brauen und seines
    Hingangs,
Des Verwesten, der bläulich die Augen aufschlägt.
O wie traurig ist dieses Wiedersehn.

IV

A high destiny ponders down Kidron passing,
Where the cedar, tender being,
Unfolds beneath the blue brows of the father,
Over the meadow at night a shepherd leads his flock.
Or there are cries in sleep
When in the grove a brazen angel advances on man
And the saint's flesh melts on the glowing grill.

Round the clay huts purple vines abound,
Sonorous sheaves of yellowed corn,
The hum of bees, the flight of the crane.
At nightfall the resurrected meet on mountain paths.

Lepers are mirrored in black waters
Or they part their filth-bespattered robes,
Weeping to the wind that blows with balm from the
    rosy hill.

Slim girls grope through the alleys of night,
To find the loving shepherd.
On Saturdays quiet singing sounds in the huts.

Let the song also remember the boy,
His madness, and white temples and his departing,
The mouldered boy, who opens bluish his eyes.
O how sorrowful is this meeting again.

V

Die Stufen des Wahnsinns in schwarzen Zimmern,
Die Schatten der Alten unter der offenen Tür,
Da Helians Seele sich im rosigen Spiegel beschaut
Und Schnee und Aussatz von seiner Stirne sinken.

An den Wänden sind die Sterne erloschen
Und die weissen Gestalten des Lichts.

Dem Teppich entsteigt Gebein der Gräber,
Das Schweigen verfallener Kreuze am Hügel,
Des Weihrauchs Süsse im purpurnen Nachtwind.

O ihr zerbrochenen Augen in schwarzen Mündern,
Da der Enkel in sanfter Umnachtung
Einsam dem dunkleren Ende nachsinnt,
Der stille Gott die blauen Lider über ihn senkt.

V

The stairs of madness in black rooms,
The shadows of the old men under the open door,
When Helian's soul regards itself in the rosy mirror
And snow and leprosy slide from his temples.

On the walls the stars have been extinguished
And the white forms of the light.

From the tapestry bones of the graves descend,
The silence of decayed crosses on the hill,
Sweetness of incense in the purple night wind.

O you crushed eyes in black mouths,
When the grandson in his mind's gentle night,
Lonely, ponders the darker ending,
The quiet god closes his blue eyelids over him.

[C.M.]

An den Knaben Elis

Elis, wenn die Amsel im schwarzen Wald ruft,
Dieses ist dein Untergang.
Deine Lippen trinken die Kühle des blauen Felsenquells.

Lass, wenn deine Stirne leise blutet
Uralte Legenden
Und dunkle Deutung des Vogelflugs.

Du aber gehst mit weichen Schritten in die Nacht,
Die voll purpurner Trauben hängt,
Und du regst die Arme schöner im Blau.

Ein Dornenbusch tönt,
Wo deine mondenen Augen sind.
O, wie lange bist, Elis, du verstorben.

Dein Leib ist eine Hyazinthe,
In die ein Mönch die wächsernen Finger taucht.
Eine schwarze Höhle ist unser Schweigen,

Daraus bisweilen ein sanftes Tier tritt
Und langsam die schweren Lider senkt.
Auf deine Schläfen tropft schwarzer Tau,

Das letzte Gold verfallener Sterne.

To the Boy Elis

Elis, when the ouzel calls in the black wood,
This is your own decline.
Your lips drink in the coolness of the blue
Spring in the rocks.

No more, when softly your forehead bleeds,
Primaeval legends
And dark interpretation of the flight of birds.

But you walk with soft footsteps into the night
Which is laden with purple grapes,
And move your arms more beautifully in the blue.

A thorn-bush sounds
Where your lunar eyes are.
O Elis, how long you have been dead.

Your body is a hyacinth
Into which a monk dips his waxen fingers.
Our silence is a black cavern

From which at times a gentle animal
Steps out and slowly lowers heavy lids.
Upon your temples black dew drips,

The last gold of perished stars.

[M.H.]

Elis

I

Vollkommen ist die Stille dieses goldenen Tags.
Unter alten Eichen
Erscheinst du, Elis, ein Ruhender mit runden Augen.

Ihre Bläue spiegelt den Schlummer der Liebenden.
An deinem Mund
Verstummten ihre rosigen Seufzer.

Am Abend zog der Fischer die schweren Netze ein.
Ein guter Hirt
Führt seine Herde am Waldsaum hin.
O! wie gerecht sind, Elis, alle deine Tage.

Leise sinkt
An kahlen Mauern des Ölbaumes blaue Stille,
Erstirbt eines Greisen dunkler Gesang.

Ein goldener Kahn
Schaukelt, Elis, dein Herz am einsamen Himmel.

II

Ein sanftes Glockenspiel tönt in Elis' Brust
Am Abend,
Da sein Haupt ins schwarze Kissen sinkt.

36

Elis

I

Absolute is the stillness of this golden day.
Under old oak trees,
Elis, you appear, one resting with round eyes.

Their blueness reflects the sleeping of lovers.
Against your mouth
Their rosy sighs died down.

At nightfall the fisherman hauled in his heavy nets.
A good shepherd
Leads his flock along the forest edge.
Oh how righteous, Elis, are all your days.

Softly sinks
The olive tree's blue stillness on bare walls,
An old man's dark song subsides.

A golden boat
Sways, Elis, your heart against a lonely sky.

II

A gentle chiming of bells resounds in Elis' breast
At nightfall,
When to the black pillow his head sinks down.

37

Ein blaues Wild
Blutet leise im Dornengestrüpp.

Ein brauner Baum steht abgeschieden da;
Seine blauen Früchte fielen von ihm.

Zeichen und Sterne
Versinken leise im Abendweiher.

Hinter dem Hügel ist es Winter geworden.

Blaue Tauben
Trinken nachts den eisigen Schweiss,
Der von Elis' kristallener Stirne rinnt.

Immer tönt
An schwarzen Mauern Gottes einsamer Wind.

A blue deer
Bleeds in the thorny thicket quietly.

Aloof and separate a brown tree stands,
Its blue fruits have fallen away.

Symbols and stars
Softly go down in the evening pond.

Behind the hill winter has come.

At night
Blue doves drink the icy sweat
That trickles from Elis' crystal brow.

Always
God's lonely wind sounds on black walls.

[M.H.]

Kindheit

Voll Früchten der Holunder; ruhig wohnte die Kindheit
In blauer Höhle. Über vergangenen Pfad,
Wo nun bräunlich das wilde Gras saust,
Sinnt das stille Geäst; das Rauschen des Laubs

Ein gleiches, wenn das blaue Wasser im Felsen tönt.
Sanft ist der Amsel Klage. Ein Hirt
Folgt sprachlos der Sonne, die vom herbstlichen Hügel rollt.

Ein blauer Augenblick ist nur mehr Seele.
Am Waldsaum zeigt sich ein scheues Wild und friedlich
Ruhn im Grund die alten Glocken und finsteren Weiler.

Frömmer kennst du den Sinn der dunklen Jahre,
Kühle und Herbst in einsamen Zimmern;
Und in heiliger Bläue läuten leuchtende Schritte fort.

Leise klirrt ein offenes Fenster; zu Tränen
Rührt der Anblick des verfallenen Friedhofs am Hügel,
Erinnerung an erzählte Legenden; doch manchmal erhellt sich die Seele,
Wenn sie frohe Menschen denkt, dunkelgoldene Frühlingstage.

Childhood

Full-berried the elder-bush; tranquilly childhood lived
In a blue cave. Over the bygone path
Where now pale brown the wild grasses hiss,
Calm branches ponder; the rustling of leaves

This too when blue waters sound under the crags.
Gentle the blackbird's plaint. A shepherd
Follows unspeaking the sun that rolls from the
autumn hill.

A blue moment is purely and simply soul.
At the forest edge a shy deer shows itself, at peace
Below in the vale the old bells and sombre hamlets
rest.

Now more devout, you know the meaning of the dark
years,
Coolness and autumn in solitary rooms;
And still in holy azure shining footfalls ring.

An open window softly knocks; tears come
At the sight of the decayed graveyard on the hill,
Memory of told legends; yet the soul sometimes
brightens
When she thinks of the glad folk, the dark-gold
springtime days.

[C.M.]

Unterwegs

Am Abend trugen sie den Fremden in die Toten-
kammer;
Ein Duft von Teer; das leise Rauschen roter Platanen;
Der dunkle Flug der Dohlen; am Platz zog eine Wache
auf.
Die Sonne ist in schwarze Linnen gesunken; immer
wieder kehrt dieser vergangene Abend.

Im Nebenzimmer spielt die Schwester eine Sonate von
Schubert.
Sehr leise sinkt ihr Lächeln in den verfallenen Brunnen,
Der bläulich in der Dämmerung rauscht. O, wie alt ist
unser Geschlecht.
Jemand flüstert drunten im Garten; jemand hat diesen
schwarzen Himmel verlassen.
Auf der Kommode duften Äpfel. Grossmutter zündet
goldene Kerzen an.

O, wie mild ist der Herbst. Leise klingen unsere
Schritte im alten Park
Unter hohen Bäumen. O, wie ernst ist das hyazinthene
Antlitz der Dämmerung.
Der blaue Quell zu deinen Füssen, geheimnisvoll die
rote Stille deines Munds,
Umdüstert vom Schlummer des Laubs, dem dunklen
Gold verfallener Sonnenblumen.

Wayfaring

At nightfall they carried the stranger dead into the
    house;
An odour of tar; the red plane trees' soft rustling;
The dark flutter of jackdaws; the guard paraded on
    the square.
The sun has sunk in black linen; time and again this
    bygone evening returns.

In the next room my sister is playing a Schubert
    sonata.
Very softly her smile sinks into the decayed fountain,
Which rustles blue in the twilight. O how old our
    family is.
Someone whispers down in the garden; someone has
    left this black heaven.
The scent of apples up on the cupboard. Grandmother
    is lighting golden candles.

O how mild the autumn is. Soft our footsteps in the
    old park
Sound under lofty trees. O how earnest is the
    hyacinthine face of twilight.
The blue spring at your feet, mysterious your mouth's
    red stillness,
Enshadowed by slumber of leaves, by the dark gold
    of decayed sunflowers.

Deine Lider sind schwer von Mohn und träumen leise
  auf meiner Stirne.
Sanfte Glocken durchzittern die Brust. Eine blaue
  Wolke
Ist dein Antlitz auf mich gesunken in der Dämmerung.

Ein Lied zur Gitarre, das in einer fremden Schenke
  erklingt,
Die wilden Holunderbüsche dort, ein lang vergangener
  Novembertag,
Vertraute Schritte auf der dämmernden Stiege, der
  Anblick gebräunter Balken,
Ein offenes Fenster, an dem ein süsses Hoffen
  zurückblieb –
Unsäglich ist das alles, o Gott, dass man erschüttert
  ins Knie bricht.

O, wie dunkel ist diese Nacht. Eine purpurne Flamme
Erlosch an meinem Mund. In der Stille
Erstirbt der bangen Seele einsames Saitenspiel.
Lass, wenn trunken von Wein das Haupt in die Gosse
  sinkt.

Your eyelids are heavy with poppy and dream softly
  against my forehead.
Gentle bells tremble through the heart. A blue cloud,
Your face has sunk over me in the twilight.

A song for the guitar, sounding in a strange tavern,
Wild elder-bushes there, a long bygone day in
  November,
Familiar steps on the dusky stair, the sight of beams
  tanned brown,
An open window, at which a sweet hope stayed
  behind –
Unspeakable it all is, O God, one is overwhelmed and
  falls on one's knees.

O how dark this night is. A purple flame
Failed at my mouth. In the stillness
The alarmed soul's lonely music fades and dies.
No more, when the wine-drunk head sinks down to
  the gutter.

                                             [C.M.]

Sebastian Im Traum

Mutter trug das Kindlein im weissen Mond,
Im Schatten des Nussbaums, uralten Holunders,
Trunken vom Safte des Mohns, der Klage der Drossel;
Und stille
Neigte in Mitleid sich über jene ein bärtiges Antlitz,

Leise im Dunkel des Fensters; und altes Hausgerät
Der Väter
Lag im Verfall; Liebe und herbstliche Träumerei.

Also dunkel der Tag des Jahrs, traurige Kindheit,
Da der Knabe leise zu kühlen Wassern, silbernen
   Fischen hinabstieg
Ruh und Antlitz;
Da er steinern sich vor rasende Rappen warf,
In grauer Nacht sein Stern über ihn kam;

Oder wenn er an der frierenden Hand der Mutter
Abends über Sankt Peters herbstlichen Friedhof ging,
Ein zarter Leichnam stille im Dunkel der Kammer lag
Und jener die kalten Lider über ihn aufhob.

46

Sebastian In Dream

Mother bore this infant in the white moon,
In the nut tree's shade, in the ancient elder's,
Drunk with the poppy's juice, the thrush's lament;
And mute
With compassion a bearded face bowed down to that
    woman,

Quiet in the window's darkness; and ancestral heir-
    looms,
Old household goods,
Lay rotting there; love and autumnal reverie.

So dark was the day of the year, desolate childhood,
When softly the boy to cool waters, to silver fishes
    walked down,
Calm and countenance;
When stony he cast himself down where black horses
    raced,
In the grey of the night his star possessed him.

Or holding his mother's icy hand
He walked at nightfall across St Peter's autumnal
    churchyard,
While a delicate corpse lay still in the bedroom's
    gloom
And he raised cold eyelids towards it.

Er aber war ein kleiner Vogel im kahlen Geäst,
Die Glocke klang im Abendnovember,
Des Vaters Stille, da er im Schlaf die dämmernde
  Wendeltreppe hinabstieg.

Frieden der Seele. Einsamer Winterabend,
Die dunklen Gestalten der Hirten am alten Weiher;
Kindlein in der Hütte von Stroh; o wie leise
Sank in schwarzem Fieber das Antlitz hin.
Heilige Nacht.

Oder wenn er an der harten Hand des Vaters
Stille den finstern Kalvarienberg hinanstieg
Und in dämmernden Felsennischen
Die blaue Gestalt des Menschen durch seine
  Legende ging,
Aus der Wunde unter dem Herzen purpurn das Blut
  rann.
O wie leise stand in dunkler Seele das Kreuz auf.

Liebe; da in schwarzen Winkeln der Schnee schmolz,
Ein blaues Lüftchen sich heiter im alten Holunder fing,
In dem Schattengewölbe des Nussbaums;
Und dem Knaben leise sein rosiger Engel erschien;

Freude; da in kühlen Zimmern eine Abendsonate
  erklang,
Im braunen Holzgebälk
Ein blauer Falter aus der silbernen Puppe kroch.

O die Nähe des Todes. In steinerner Mauer
Neigte sich ein gelbes Haupt, schweigend das Kind,
Da in jenem März der Mond verfiel.

But he was a little bird in leafless boughs,
The churchbell rang in dusking November,
His father's stillness, when asleep he descended the
    dark of the turning stair.

Peace of the soul. A lonely winter evening.
The dark shapes of shepherds by the ancient pond;
Little child in the hut of straw; O how softly
Into black fever his face sank down.
Holy night.

Or holding his father's horny hand
In silence he walked up Calvary Hill
And in dusky rock recesses
The blue shape of Man would pass through His legend,
Blood ran purple from the wound beneath His heart.
O how softly the Cross rose up in the dark of his soul.

Love; when in black corners the snow was melting,
Gaily a little blue breeze was caught in the ancient
    elder,
In the nut tree's vault of shade;
And in silence a rosy angel appeared to that boy;

Gladness; when in cool rooms a sonata sounded at
    nightfall,
Among dark-brown beams
A blue butterfly crept from its silver chrysalis.

O the nearness of death. From the stony wall
A yellow head bowed down, silent that child,
Since in that month the moon decayed.

Rosige Osterglocke im Grabgewölbe der Nacht
Und die Silberstimmen der Sterne,
Dass in Schauern ein dunkler Wahnsinn von der Stirne
    des Schläfers sank.

O wie stille ein Gang den blauen Fluss hinab
Vergessenes sinnend, da im grünen Geäst
Die Drossel ein Fremdes in den Untergang rief.

Oder wenn er an der knöchernen Hand des Greisen
Abends vor die verfallene Mauer der Stadt ging
Und jener in schwarzem Mantel ein rosiges Kindlein
    trug,
Im Schatten des Nussbaums der Geist des Bösen
    erschien.

Tasten über die grünen Stufen des Sommers. O wie
    leise
Verlief der Garten in der braunen Stille des Herbstes,
Duft und Schwermut des alten Holunders,
Da in Sebastians Schatten die Silberstimme des Engels
    erstarb.

Rose-coloured Easter bell in the burial vault of the
  night,
And the silver voices of stars,
So that madness, dark and shuddering, ebbed from the
  sleeper's brow.

O how quiet to ramble along the blue river's bank,
To ponder forgotten things when in leafy boughs
The thrush's call brought strangeness into a world's
  decline.

Or holding an old man's bony hand
In the evening he walked to the crumbling city walls,
And in his black greatcoat carried a rosy child,
In the nut tree's shade the spirit of evil appeared.

Groping his way over the green steps of summer. O
  how softly
In autumn's brown stillness the garden decayed,
Scent and sadness of the ancient elder,
When the silver voice of the angel died down in
  Sebastian's shadow.

[M.H.]

Nachtlied

Des Unbewegten Odem. Ein Tiergesicht
Erstarrt vor Bläue, ihrer Heiligkeit.
Gewaltig ist das Schweigen im Stein.

Die Maske eines nächtlichen Vogels. Sanfter Dreiklang
Verklingt in einem. Elai! dein Antlitz
Beugt sich sprachlos über bläuliche Wasser.

O! ihr stillen Spiegel der Wahrheit.
An des Einsamen elfenbeinerner Schläfe
Erscheint der Abglanz gefallener Engel.

Nocturne

Breath of the One Unmoved. Animal face
Frozen with azure, with its sanctity.
Immense the power of silence in stone.

The mask of a night bird. A quiet triad
Fades on one sound. Elai! your countenance
Inclines unspeaking over the pale-blue waters.

O you calm mirrors of the truth.
On the ivory cheeks of the lonely one appears
Reflected the splendour of fallen angels.

[C.M.]

Am Moor

Wanderer im schwarzen Wind; leise flüstert das dürre
  Rohr
In der Stille des Moors. Am grauen Himmel
Ein Zug von wilden Vögeln folgt;
Quere über finsteren Wassern.

Aufruhr. In verfallener Hütte
Aufflattert mit schwarzen Flügeln die Fäulnis;
Verkrüppelte Birken seufzen im Wind.

Abend in verlassener Schenke. Den Heimweg
  umwittert
Die sanfte Schwermut grasender Herden,
Erscheinung der Nacht : Kröten tauchen aus silbernen
  Wassern.

On the Moors

Wanderer in black wind; lightly the dry reed
Whispers in the stillness of the moor. Under grey
  heavens
A flight of wild birds passes,
Crosswise, over dark water.

Uproar. In ruined cottages
On black wings, foulness flaps up;
Crippled birches creak in the wind.

Evening in the abandoned tavern. The gentle melan-
  choly
Of grazing herds encloses the way home,
Apparition of Night: toads plunge out of silvery
  waters.

[R.G.]

Am Mönchsberg

Wo im Schatten herbstlicher Ulmen der verfallene
   Pfad hinabsinkt,
Ferne den Hütten von Laub, schlafenden Hirten,
Immer folgt dem Wandrer die dunkle Gestalt der
   Kühle

Über knöchernen Steg, die hyazinthene Stimme des
   Knaben,
Leise sagend die vergessene Legende des Walds,
Sanfter ein Krankes nun die wilde Klage des Bruders.

Also rührt ein spärliches Grün das Knie des Fremd-
   lings,
Das versteinerte Haupt;
Näher rauscht der blaue Quell die Klage der Frauen.

On the Mönchsberg

Where the crumbling pathway descends in the shadow
   of autumn elms,
Far from the leafy huts, the sleeping shepherds,
The dark shape that came from the coolness still
   follows the wanderer

Over the footbridge of bone, and the boy's hyacinth
   voice
Softly reciting the forest's forgotten legend,
And more gently, a sick thing now, the brother's wild
   lament.

Thus a little green touches the knee of the stranger,
And his head that turned to stone;
Nearer, the blue spring murmurs the women's
   lamentation.

[D.L.]

Kaspar Hauser Lied
Für Bessie Loos

Er wahrlich liebte die Sonne, die purpurn den Hügel
  hinabstieg,
Die Wege des Walds, den singenden Schwarzvogel
Und die Freude des Grüns.

Ernsthaft war sein Wohnen im Schatten des Baums
Und rein sein Antlitz.
Gott sprach eine sanfte Flamme zu seinem Herzen:
O Mensch!

Stille fand sein Schritt die Stadt am Abend;
Die dunkle Klage seines Munds:
Ich will ein Reiter werden.

Ihm aber folgte Busch und Tier,
Haus und Dämmergarten weisser Menschen
Und sein Mörder suchte nach ihm.

Frühling und Sommer und schön der Herbst
Des Gerechten, sein leiser Schritt
And den dunklen Zimmern Träumender hin.
Nachts blieb er mit seinem Stern allein;

Sah, dass Schnee fiel in kahles Gezweig
Und im dämmernden Hausflur den Schatten des
  Mörders.

Silbern sank des Ungebornen Haupt hin.

Caspar Hauser Song
For Bessie Loos

He truly adored the sun, as, crimson, it sank from the
    hill-top,
The paths of the forest, the blackbird singing
And the joy of green.

Serious was his habitation in the tree-shade
And pure his face.
God spoke a gentle flame into his heart:
O man!

His silent footstep found the city at evening;
The dark lament of his mouth:
I want to be a horseman.

But bush and beast pursued him,
House and twilit garden of pallid men
And his murderer sought him.

Beautiful the spring and summer and the autumn
Of the righteous man, his soft footfall
Beside the dark rooms of dreamers.
By night he stayed alone with his star;

Saw snow falling through bare branches
And in the dusking hall his murderer's shadow.

Silver it fell, the head of the not-yet-born.

[D.L.]

Entlang

Geschnitten sind Korn und Traube,
Der Weiler in Herbst und Ruh.
Hammer und Amboss klingt immerzu,
Lachen in purpurner Laube.

Astern von dunklen Zäunen
Bring dem weissen Kind.
Sag wie lang wir gestorben sind;
Sonne will schwarz erscheinen.

Rotes Fischlein im Weiher;
Stirn, die sich fürchtig belauscht;
Abendwind leise ans Fenster rauscht,
Blaues Orgelgeleier.

Stern und heimlich Gefunkel
Lässt noch einmal aufschaun.
Erscheinung der Mutter in Schmerz und Graun;
Schwarze Reseden im Dunkel.

In Transit

Grain and grape have been cut,
The hamlet in autumn and peace.
Hammer and anvil clang incessantly,
Laughter in purple leaves.

Asters past dark hedges
Summon the pale child.
Say how long it is we have been dead;
The sun desires to shine black.

Little red fish in the fishpond;
Forehead, afraid, overhearing itself;
Evening wind against the window delicately rustles,
Blue organ grinding.

Secret sparkle of stars
Lets one look up once more.
Apparition of the mother in pain and horror;
Black mignonettes in the dark.

[R.G.]

Der Herbst des Einsamen

Der dunkle Herbst kehrt ein voll Frucht und Fülle,
Vergilbter Glanz von schönen Sommertagen.
Ein reines Blau tritt aus verfallner Hülle;
Der Flug der Vögel tönt von alten Sagen.
Gekeltert ist der Wein, die milde Stille
Erfüllt von leiser Antwort dunkler Fragen.

Und hier und dort ein Kreuz auf ödem Hügel;
Im roten Wald verliert sich eine Herde.
Die Wolke wandert übern Weiherspiegel;
Es ruht des Landmanns ruhige Gebärde.
Sehr leise rührt des Abends blauer Flügel
Ein Dach von dürrem Stroh, die schwarze Erde.

Bald nisten Sterne in des Müden Brauen;
In kühle Stuben kehrt ein still Bescheiden
Und Engel treten leise aus den blauen
Augen der Liebenden, die sanfter leiden.
Es rauscht das Rohr; anfällt ein knöchern Grauen,
Wenn schwarz der Tau tropft von den kahlen Weiden.

The Fall of the Lonely One

Again dark fall returns, replete with fruit, profusion,
The yellowed sheen of lovely summer days.
A clear blue steps from rotting husks;
The flight of birds whirrs with ancient myths.
Now wine's pressed, the mild stillness
Is filled with low-voiced answers to dark questions.

And here and there a cross upon a wasted hill; a herd
Disperses into red woods. Over the fishpond's
Mirror surface strays a cloud;
The farmer's quiet gesture is at rest.
So gently the blue flight of evening stirs,
A roof of dry straw, black earth.

Soon stars nestle in the tired one's eyebrows;
A quiet modesty in cool rooms faces about
And angels stalk noiselessly out of the blue
Eyes of lovers, who more gently suffer.
A rustling of reeds; a bony horror attacks
As black dew drips from bare willow boughs.

[R.G.]

Ruh und Schweigen

Hirten begruben die Sonne im kahlen Wald.
Ein Fischer zog
In härenem Netz den Mond aus frierendem Weiher.

In blauem Kristall
Wohnt der bleiche Mensch, die Wang' an seine
    Sterne gelehnt;
Oder er neigt das Haupt in purpurnem Schlaf.

Doch immer rührt der schwarze Flug der Vögel
Den Schauenden, das Heilige blauer Blumen,
Denkt die nahe Stille Vergessenes, erloschene Engel.

Wieder nachtet die Stirne in mondenem Gestein;
Ein strahlender Jüngling
Erscheint die Schwester in Herbst und schwarzer
    Verwesung.

Rest and Silence

Shepherds have buried the sun in the bare forest.
A fisherman has hauled
The moon in a fine-spun net from the freezing pond.

In a blue crystal,
Pallid, man dwells, and his cheek leans on his stars;
Or he bows his head in purple sleep.

Yet still by birds' black flight the visionary
Is touched, and by blue flowers' holiness,
And the near-by silence ponders forgotten things,
     extinguished angels.

Night envelops the brow once more amid lunar stones;
And a radiant youth
The sister appears amid autumn and black corruption.
                                                    [D.L.]

Geburt

Gebirge : Schwärze, Schweigen und Schnee.
Rot vom Wald niedersteigt die Jagd;
O, die moosigen Blicke des Wilds.

Stille der Mutter; unter schwarzen Tannen
Öffnen sich die schlafenden Hände,
Wenn verfallen der kalte Mond erscheint.

O, die Geburt des Menschen. Nächtlich rauscht
Blaues Wasser im Felsengrund;
Seufzend erblickt sein Bild der gefallene Engel,

Erwacht ein Bleiches in dumpfer Stube.
Zwei Monde
Erglänzen die Augen der steinernen Greisin.

Weh, der Gebärenden Schrei. Mit schwarzem Flügel
Rührt die Knabenschläfe die Nacht,
Schnee, der leise aus purpurner Wolke sinkt.

Birth

Mountains: blackness, silence and snow,
Red from the forest the hunt comes down;
O the mossy gaze of the wild deer.

The mother's stillness; under black pine trees
The sleeping hands extending open
When the cold moon appears in its decay.

O the birth of man. Nocturnal murmur
Blue waters rushing over the rock-bed;
Sighing the fallen angel espies his image,

Something pale wakes in a musty room.
Two moons,
The old stone woman's eyes are shining.

Ah how the mother cries in labour. With black wing
Night brushes the boy's cheek,
Snow that softly from purple cloud descends.

[C.M.]

Untergang
An Karl Borromäus Heinrich

Über den weissen Weiher
Sind die wilden Vögel fortgezogen.
Am Abend weht von unseren Sternen ein eisiger Wind.

Über unsere Gräber
Beugt sich die zerbrochene Stirne der Nacht.
Unter Eichen schaukeln wir auf einem silbernen Kahn.

Immer klingen die weissen Mauern der Stadt.
Unter Dornenbogen
O mein Bruder klimmen wir blinde Zeiger gen
    Mitternacht.

Decline

To Karl Borromäus Heinrich

Over the white pond
The wild birds have travelled on.
In the evening an icy wind blows from our stars.

Over our graves
The broken brow of the night inclines.
Under oak trees we sway in a silver boat.

Always the town's white walls resound.
Under arches of thorns,
O my brother, blind minute-hands,
We climb towards midnight.

[M.H.]

An Einen Frühverstorbenen

O, der schwarze Engel, der leise aus dem Innern des
  Baums trat,
Da wir sanfte Gespielen am Abend waren,
Am Rand des bläulichen Brunnens.
Ruhig war unser Schritt, die runden Augen in der
  braunen Kühle des Herbstes,
O, die purpurne Süsse der Sterne.

Jener aber ging die steinernen Stufen des Mönchsbergs
  hinab,
Ein blaues Lächeln im Antlitz und seltsam verpuppt
In seine stillere Kindheit und starb;
Und im Garten blieb das silberne Antlitz des Freundes
  zurück,
Lauschend im Laub oder im alten Gestein.

Seele sang den Tod, die grüne Verwesung des Fleisches
Und es war das Rauschen des Walds,
Die inbrünstige Klage des Wildes.
Immer klangen von dämmernden Türmen die blauen
  Glocken des Abends.

Stunde kam, da jener die Schatten in purpurner Sonne
  sah,
Die Schatten der Fäulnis in kahlem Geäst;
Abend, da an dämmernder Mauer die Amsel sang,
Der Geist des Frühverstorbenen stille im Zimmer
  erschien.

To One Who Died Young

O the black angel who softly stepped from the heart of
   the tree
When we were gentle playmates in the evening,
By the edge of the pale-blue fountain.
Our step was easy, the round eyes in autumn's brown
   coolness,
O the purple sweetness of the stars.

But the other descended the stone steps of the
   Mönchsberg,
A blue smile on his face, and strangely ensheathed
In his quieter childhood, and died;
And the silver face of his friend stayed behind in the
   garden,
Listening in the leaves or in the ancient stones.

Soul sang of death, the green decay of the flesh,
And it was the murmur of the forest,
The fervid lament of the animals.
Always from dusky towers rang the blue evening
   bells.

Times came when the other saw shadows in the purple
   sun,
The shadows of putrescence in the bare branches;
At evening, when by the dusky wall the blackbird
   sang,
His ghost quietly appeared there in the room.

O, das Blut, das aus der Kehle des Tönenden rinnt,
Blaue Blume; o die feurige Träne
Geweint in die Nacht.

Goldene Wolke und Zeit. In einsamer Kammer
Lädst du öfter den Toten zu Gast,
Wandelst in trautem Gespräch unter Ulmen den
  grünen Fluss hinab.

O the blood that runs from the throat of the musical
    one,
Blue flower; O the fiery tear
Wept into the night.

Golden cloud and time. In a lonely room
You ask the dead child to visit you more often,
You walk and talk together under elms by the green
    riverside.

                                      [C.M.]

Abendländisches Lied

O der Seele nächtlicher Flügelschlag:
Hirten gingen wir einst an dämmernden Wäldern hin
Und es folgte das rote Wild, die grüne Blume und der
    lallende Quell
Demutsvoll. O, der uralte Ton des Heimchens,
Blut blühend am Opferstein
Und der Schrei des einsamen Vogels über der grünen
    Stille des Teichs.

O, ihr Kreuzzüge und glühenden Martern
Des Fleisches, Fallen purpurner Früchte
Im Abendgarten, wo vor Zeiten die frommen Jünger
    gegangen,
Kriegsleute nun, erwachend aus Wunden und
    Sternenträumen.
O, das sanfte Zyanenbündel der Nacht.

O, ihr Zeiten der Stille und goldener Herbste,
Da wir friedliche Mönche die purpurne Traube
    gekeltert;
Und rings erglänzten Hügel und Wald.
O, ihr Jagden und Schlösser; Ruh des Abends,
Da in seiner Kammer der Mensch Gerechtes sann,
In stummem Gebet um Gottes lebendiges Haupt rang.

Western Song

O the soul's nocturnal wingbeat:
Shepherds we walked by dusky forests once
And the red deer followed, the green flower and
  babbling stream,
Humbly. O the ancient sound of the little home,
Blood flowering on the sacrificial slab
And the lonely birdcry over the pond's green calm.

O you crusades and glowing tortures
Of the flesh, descent of the crimson fruits
In the garden at evening where long ago the pious
  disciples walked,
People now of war, from wounds and star-dreams
  waking.
O the gentle cornflower sheaf of night.

O you times of quietness and golden autumns
When peaceful monks we trod the purple grape;
And hill and forest shone around us.
O you hunts and castles; peace at evening,
When in his room man meditated justice,
Wrestled in dumb prayer for the living head of God.

O, die bittere Stunde des Untergangs,
Da wir ein steinernes Antlitz in schwarzen Wassern
    beschaun.
Aber strahlend heben die silbernen Lider die
    Liebenden :
Ein Geschlecht. Weihrauch strömt von rosigen Kissen
Und der süsse Gesang der Auferstandenen.

O the bitter hour of decline,
When we regard a stony face in black waters.
But radiant the lovers raise their silver eyelids:
One kin. From rosy pillows incense pours
And the sweet canticle of the bodies resurrected.

[C.M.]

Föhn

Blinde Klage im Wind, mondene Wintertage,
Kindheit, leise verhallen die Schritte an schwarzer
 Hecke,
Langes Abendgeläut.
Leise kommt die weisse Nacht gezogen,

Verwandelt in purpurne Träume Schmerz und Plage
Des steinigen Lebens,
Dass nimmer der dornige Stachel ablasse vom ver-
 wesenden Leib.

Tief im Schlummer aufseufzt die bange Seele,

Tief der Wind in zerbrochenen Bäumen,
Und es schwankt die Klagegestalt
Der Mutter durch den einsamen Wald

Dieser schweigenden Trauer; Nächte,
Erfüllt von Tränen, feurigen Engeln.
Silbern zerschellt an kahler Mauer ein kindlich
 Gerippe.

South Wind

Blind lamentation in the wind, moon-days of winter,
Childhood, softly footsteps fade by the dark hedge,
The long peal of bells in the evening.
Softly the pallid night approaches,

Transforms into purple dreams the pain and affliction
Of stony life,
That without abatement the thorn may goad the
decaying body.

From the depths of its sleep the fear-stricken soul
moans suddenly,

And the wind in the depths of broken trees,
And swaying, a shape of lamentation,
The mother moves through the lonely wood

Of this speechless grief; nights
Full of tears, nights full of fiery angels.
Silver, against a bare wall, a child's skeleton smashes.

[D.L.]

An die Verstummten

O, der Wahnsinn der grossen Stadt, da am Abend
An schwarzer Mauer verkrüppelte Bäume starren,
Aus silberner Maske der Geist des Bösen schaut;
Licht mit magnetischer Geissel die steinerne Nacht
    verdrängt.
O, das versunkene Läuten der Abendglocken.

Hure, die in eisigen Schauern ein totes Kindlein gebärt.
Rasend peitscht Gottes Zorn die Stirn des Besessenen,
Purpurne Seuche, Hunger, der grüne Augen zerbricht.
O, das grässliche Lachen des Golds.

Aber stille blutet in dunkler Höhle stummere Mensch-
    heit,
Fügt aus harten Metallen das erlösende Haupt.

To the Silenced

Oh, the great city's madness when at nightfall
The crippled trees gape by the blackened wall,
The spirit of evil peers from a silver mask;
Lights with magnetic scourge drive off the stony night.
Oh, the sunken pealing of evening bells.

Whore who in her icy spasms gives birth to a dead
child.
With raving whips God's fury punishes brows pos-
sessed.
Purple pestilence, hunger that breaks green eyes.
Oh, the horrible laughter of gold.

But silent in dark caves a stiller humanity bleeds,
Out of hard metals moulds the redeeming head.

[M.H.]

Vorhölle

An herbstlichen Mauern, es suchen Schatten dort
Am Hügel das tönende Gold
Weidende Abendwolken
In der Ruh verdorrter Platanen.
Dunklere Tränen odmet diese Zeit,
Verdammnis, da des Träumers Herz
Überfliesst von purpurner Abendröte,
Der Schwermut der rauchenden Stadt;
Dem Schreitenden nachweht goldene Kühle,
Dem Fremdling, vom Friedhof,
Als folgte im Schatten ein zarter Leichnam.

Leise läutet der steinerne Bau;
Der Garten der Waisen, das dunkle Spital,
Ein rotes Schiff am Kanal.
Träumend steigen und sinken im Dunkel
Verwesende Menschen
Und aus schwärzlichen Toren
Treten Engel mit kalten Stirnen hervor;
Bläue, die Todesklagen der Mütter.
Es rollt durch ihr langes Haar,
Ein feuriges Rad, der runde Tag
Der Erde Qual ohne Ende.

In kühlen Zimmern ohne Sinn
Modert Gerät, mit knöchernen Händen
Tastet im Blau nach Märchen

Limbo

By autumnal walls, shadows are searching there
For singing gold on the hill
Evening clouds that browse
In the withered plane trees' calm.
Darker tears this age exhales,
Perdition, when the dreamer's heart
Is overflowing with purple sunset,
With the dejection of the smoking town;
Golden cool blows from behind the traveller,
The stranger, from the graveyard,
As if a delicate corpse were shadowing him.

The stone building softly chimes;
The orphans' garden, the dark hospital,
A red ship on the canal.
Decaying men
Dreaming rise and fall in the dark
And from blackish doorways
Angels advance with cold foreheads;
Azure, the keening of mothers.
There rolls through her long hair
A fiery wheel, the round day,
Unending torture of the earth.

In cool rooms, without meaning,
Furniture rots, with bony hands
Unholy childhood

Unheilige Kindheit,
Benagt die fette Ratte Tür und Truh,
Ein Herz
Erstarrt in schneeiger Stille.
Nachhallen die purpurnen Flüche
Des Hungers in faulendem Dunkel,
Die schwarzen Schwerter der Lüge,
Als schlüge zusammen ein ehernes Tor.

Fumbles in the blue for fairytales,
The plump rat gnaws cupboard and door,
A heart
Stiffens in snowy silence.
Echoes resound in decaying darkness,
The purple curses of hunger echoing,
The dark sword-blades of lies,
As if somewhere a brazen gate had slammed.

[C.M.]

Die Sonne

Täglich kommt die gelbe Sonne über den Hügel.
Schön ist der Wald, das dunkle Tier,
Der Mensch; Jäger oder Hirt.

Rötlich steigt im grünen Weiher der Fisch.
Unter dem runden Himmel
Fährt der Fischer leise im blauen Kahn.

Langsam reift die Traube, das Korn.
Wenn sich stille der Tag neigt,
Ist ein Gutes und Böses bereitet.

Wenn es Nacht wird,
Hebt der Wanderer leise die schweren Lider;
Sonne aus finsterer Schlucht bricht.

The Sun

Daily the yellow sun comes over the hill.
Lovely the forest is, the dark beast,
And man : huntsman or shepherd.

Ruddy the fish rises in the green pond.
Under the rounded heaven
The fisherman softly moves in a blue boat.

Grape ripens slowly, and the corn.
As day in stillness ends,
A good work and an evil is prepared.

When night comes,
The wanderer softly lifts his heavy eyelids.
Sun breaks from a sombre abyss.

[C.M.]

Sommer

Am Abend schweigt die Klage
Des Kuckucks im Wald.
Tiefer neigt sich das Korn,
Der rote Mohn.

Schwarzes Gewitter droht
Über dem Hügel.
Das alte Lied der Grille
Erstirbt im Feld.

Nimmer regt sich das Laub
Der Kastanie.
Auf der Wendeltreppe
Rauscht dein Kleid.

Stille leuchtet die Kerze
Im dunklen Zimmer;
Eine silberne Hand
Löschte sie aus;

Windstille, sternlose Nacht.

Summer

At evening, the sound of the cuckoo
Stops in the wood.
The grain bends lower,
The red poppy.

Black thunderclouds bloom
Above the hill.
The ancient song of the cricket
Fades off into the fields.

The leaves of the chestnut
Tree stir no more.
Upon the spiral staircase
Your dress rustles.

One silent candle shines
In the dark room;
A silvery hand
Extinguishes it;

No wind, no stars. Night.

[R.G.]

Abendland

Else Lasker-Schüler in Verehrung

I

Mond, als träte ein Totes
Aus blauer Höhle,
Und es fallen der Blüten
Viele über den Felsenpfad.
Silbern weint ein Krankes
Am Abendweiher,
Auf schwarzem Kahn
Hinüberstarben Liebende.

Oder es läuten die Schritte
Elis' durch den Hain
Den hyazinthenen
Wieder verhallend unter Eichen.
O des Knaben Gestalt
Geformt aus kristallenen Tränen,
Nächtigen Schatten.
Zackige Blitze erhellen die Schläfe
Die immerkühle,
Wenn am grünenden Hügel
Frühlingsgewitter ertönt.

Occident

For Else Lasker-Schüler

I

Moon, as if a dead thing
Stepped out of a blue cave,
And many blossoms fall
Across the rocky path.
Silver a sick thing weeps
By the evening pond,
In a black boat
Lovers crossed over to death

Or the footsteps of Elis
Ring through the grove
The hyacinthine
To fade again under oaks.
O the shape of that boy
Formed out of crystal tears,
Nocturnal shadows.
Jagged lightning illumines his temples
The ever-cool,
When on the verdant hill
Springtime thunder resounds.

II

So leise sind die grünen Wälder
Unserer Heimat,
Die kristallne Woge
Hinsterbend an verfallner Mauer
Und wir haben im Schlaf geweint;
Wandern mit zögernden Schritten
An der dornigen Hecke hin
Singende im Abendsommer
In heiliger Ruh
Des fern verstrahlenden Weinbergs;
Schatten nun im kühlen Schoss
Der Nacht, trauernde Adler.
So leise schliesst ein mondener Strahl
Die purpurnen Male der Schwermut.

III

Ihr grossen Städte
steinern aufgebaut
in der Ebene!
So sprachlos folgt
der Heimatlose
mit dunkler Stirne dem Wind,
kahlen Bäumen am Hügel.
Ihr weithin dämmernden Ströme!
Gewaltig ängstet
schaurige Abendröte
im Sturmgewölk.
Ihr sterbenden Völker!
Bleiche Woge
zerschellend am Strande der Nacht,
fallende Sterne.

II

So quiet are the green woods
Of our homeland,
The crystal wave
That dies against a perished wall
And we have wept in our sleep;
Wander with hesitant steps
Along the thorny hedge
Singers in the evening summer
In holy peace
Of the vineyards distantly gleaming;
Shadows now in the cool lap
Of night, eagles that mourn.
So quietly does a moonbeam close
The purple wounds of sadness.

III

You mighty cities
stone on stone raised up
in the plain!
So quietly
with darkened forehead
the outcast follows the wind,
bare trees on the hillside.
You rivers distantly fading!
Gruesome sunset red
is breeding fear
in the thunderclouds.
You dying peoples!
Pallid billow
that breaks on the beaches of Night,
stars that are falling.

[M.H.]

Frühling der Seele

Aufschrei im Schlaf; durch schwarze Gassen stürzt
    der Wind,
Das Blau des Frühlings winkt durch brechendes
    Geäst,
Purpurner Nachttau und es erlöschen rings die Sterne.
Grünlich dämmert der Fluss, silbern die alten Alleen
Und die Türme der Stadt. O sanfte Trunkenheit
Im gleitenden Kahn und die dunklen Rufe der Amsel
In kindlichen Gärten. Schon lichtet sich der rosige Flor.

Feierlich rauschen die Wasser. O die feuchten
    Schatten der Au,
Das schreitende Tier; Grünendes, Blütengezweig
Rührt die kristallene Stirne; schimmernder Schaukel-
    kahn.
Leist tönt die Sonne im Rosengewölk am Hügel.
Gross ist die Stille des Tannenwalds, die ernsten
    Schatten am Fluss.

Reinheit! Reinheit! Wo sind die furchtbaren Pfade
    des Todes,
Des grauen steinernen Schweigens, die Felsen der
    Nacht
Und die friedlosen Schatten? Strahlender Sonnenab-
    grund.

The Soul's Springtime

A sudden cry in sleep; wind rushes through dark
    streets,
Azure of spring beckons through breaking branches,
Night's dew is purple, stars all round the sky are
    fading.
The river gleams green in the dusk, and silver the old
    avenues
And the spires of the city. O gentle drunkenness
In the gliding boat, O the dark calls of blackbirds
In childlike gardens. The rose-red veil disperses.

Solemnly the waters murmur. O the moist shadows on
    the meadow,
The animals walking; green things, a spray of blossoms
Touching the crystal brow; shimmering rocking boat.
Softly the sun sings through the rose-red clouds on the
    hill.
Great is the stillness of the pinewood, grave the
    shadows by the river.

Purity! Purity! Where are the terrible pathways of
    death,
Of grey stony silence, the rocks of the night
And the unquiet shades? A radiant pit of sunlight.

Schwester, da ich dich fand an einsamer Lichtung
Des Waldes und Mittag war und gross das Schweigen
    des Tiers;
Weisse unter wilder Eiche, und es blühte silbern der
    Dorn.
Gewaltiges Sterben und die singende Flamme im
    Herzen.

Dunkler umfliessen die Wasser die schönen Spiele der
    Fische.
Stunde der Trauer, schweigender Anblick der Sonne;
Es ist die Seele ein Fremdes auf Erden. Geistlich
    dämmert
Bläue über dem verhauenen Wald und es läutet
Lange eine dunkle Glocke im Dorf; friedlich Geleit.
Stille blüht die Myrthe über den weissen Lidern des
    Toten.

Leise tönen die Wasser im sinkenden Nachmittag
Und es grünet dunkler die Wildnis am Ufer, Freude im
    rosigen Wind;
Der sanfte Gesang des Bruders am Abendhügel.

O my sister, when I found you by the lonely clearing
In the wood, at noon, in a great silence of all animals,
You were white under the wild oak, and the silver
    thorn-bush blossomed.
A mighty dying, and the singing flame in the heart.

Darker the waters flow round the fishes gracefully
    playing.
O hour of grief, O speechless gaze of the sun.
The soul is an alien thing upon earth. A dim religious
Azure descends on the mishewn forest, and a bell
Tolls from the village dark and long; they lead him to
    rest.
Silent the myrtle blooms over his dead white eyelids.

Softly the waters murmur in the declining afternoon.
On the river bank the green wilderness darkens, the
    rose-red wind rejoices;
A brother's gentle song on the evening hill.

[D.L.]

Winternacht

Es ist Schnee gefallen. Nach Mitternacht verlässt du betrunken von purpurnem Wein den dunklen Bezirk der Menschen, die rote Flamme ihres Herdes. O die Finsternis!

Schwarzer Frost. Die Erde ist hart, nach Bitterem schmeckt die Luft. Deine Sterne schliessen sich zu bösen Zeichen.

Mit versteinerten Schritten stampfst du am Bahndamm hin, mit runden Augen, wie ein Soldat, der eine schwarze Schanze stürmt. Avanti!

Bitterer Schnee und Mond!

Ein roter Wolf, den ein Engel würgt. Deine Beine klirren schreitend wie blaues Eis und ein Lächeln voll Trauer und Hochmut hat dein Antlitz versteinert und die Stirne erbleicht vor der Wollust des Frostes;

oder sie neigt sich schweigend über den Schlaf eines Wächters, der in seiner hölzernen Hütte hinsank.

Frost und Rauch. Ein weisses Sternenhemd verbrennt die tragenden Schultern und Gottes Geier zerfleischen dein metallenes Herz.

O der steinerne Hügel. Stille schmilzt und vergessen der kühle Leib im silbernen Schnee hin.

Schwarz ist der Schlaf. Das Ohr folgt lange den Pfaden der Sterne im Eis.

Beim Erwachen klangen die Glocken im Dorf. Aus dem östlichen Tor trat silbern der rosige Tag.

Winter Night

Snow has been falling. After midnight, drunk with purple wine, you leave the dark district of men, the red flame of their hearth-fires. O darkness!

Black frost. The earth is hard, the air tastes of bitterness. Your stars conjoin to evil signs.

With petrified steps you stamp along the railway-track, with rounded eyes, like a soldier storming a black redoubt. Avanti!

Bitter snow and moon!

A red wolf strangled by an angel. Your walking legs clash like blue ice and a smile full of sadness and pride has petrified your face and your brow grows pale with the voluptuous frost;

or silently stoops over the sleep of a watchman who lay down in his wooden hut.

Frost and smoke. A white shirt of stars burns the shoulders that wear it, and God's vultures tear the flesh of your metal heart.

O the stone hill. Silent and forgotten, the cool body melts away in the silver snow.

The blackness of sleep. Far through the ice the ear follows the paths of the stars.

When you woke, the bells in the village were ringing. The rose-red silver day stepped through the eastern gate.

[D.L.]

In Hellbrunn

Wieder folgend der blauen Klage des Abends
Am Hügel hin, am Frühlingsweiher –
Als schwebten darüber die Schatten lange Verstor-
   bener,
Die Schatten der Kirchenfürsten, edler Frauen –
Schon blühen ihre Blumen, die ernsten Veilchen
Im Abendgrund, rauscht des blauen Quells
Kristallne Woge. So geistlich ergrünen
Die Eichen über den vergessenen Pfaden der Toten,
Die goldene Wolke über dem Weiher.

In Hellbrunn

Following once again the evening's blue lament
Along the hillside, along the vernal pond –
As if the shades of those long dead, the shades
Of prelates and of noble women hovered over them –
Their flowers are blooming already, the earnest violets
In the evening's depth, the blue wellspring's
Crystal wave purls on. So religiously
Do the oaks grow green over forgotten paths of the
    dead,
The golden cloud over the pond.

[M.H.]

Das Herz

Das wilde Herz ward weiss am Wald;
O dunkle Angst
Des Todes, so das Gold
In grauer Wolke starb.
Novemberabend.
Am kahlen Tor am Schlachthaus stand
Der armen Frauen Schar;
In jeden Korb
Fiel faules Fleisch und Eingeweid;
Verfluchte Kost!

Des Abends blaue Taube
Brachte nicht Versöhnung.
Dunkler Trompetenruf
Durchfuhr der Ulmen
Nasses Goldlaub,
Eine zerfetzte Fahne
Vom Blute rauchend,
Dass in wilder Schwermut
Hinlauscht ein Mann.
O! ihr ehernen Zeiten
Begraben dort im Abendrot.

Aus dunklem Hausflur trat
Die goldne Gestalt
Der Jünglingin
Umgeben von bleichen Monden,

The Heart

The wild heart turned white in the wood;
O the dark fear
Of death, when the gold
Died in a grey cloud.
November evening.
By the bare gate of the slaughterhouse there stood
The crowd of poor women.
Into every basket
Rank flesh and entrails fell;
Accursed fare!

The blue dove of nightfall
Brought no atonement.
Dark trumpet call
Rang through the elm trees'
Damp golden leaves,
A tattered banner
Steaming with blood,
So that wild in his sadness
A man gives heed.
O brazen ages
Buried there in the sunset red.

From the house's dark hall there stepped
The golden shape
Of the maiden-youth
Surrounded with pale moons

Herbstlicher Hofstaat,
Zerknickten schwarze Tannen
Im Nachtsturm,
Die steile Festung.
O Herz
Hinüberschimmernd in schneeige Kühle.

Of autumnal courtliness,
Black pine trees snapped
In the night gale,
The steep-walled fortress.
O heart
Glistening away into snowy coolness.

[M.H.]

Der Schlaf

Verflucht ihr dunklen Gifte,
Weisser Schlaf!
Dieser höchst seltsame Garten
Dämmernder Bäume
Erfüllt von Schlangen, Nachtfaltern,
Spinnen, Fledermäusen.
Fremdling! Dein verlorner Schatten
Im Abendrot,
Ein finsterer Korsar
Im salzigen Meer der Trübsal.
Aufflattern weisse Vögel am Nachtsaum
Über stürzenden Städten
Von Stahl.

Sleep

Accursed you dark poisons,
White sleep!
This, the rarest of gardens
Of trees wrapped in twilight,
Filled with serpents, nocturnal moths,
Spiders and bats.
Stranger, your lost shadow
In the sunset's red,
A gloomy corsair
On the salt sea of sadness.
White birds on the hem of the night fly off
Over collapsing cities
Of steel.

[M.H.]

Der Abend

Mit toten Heldengestalten
Erfüllst du Mond
Die schweigenden Wälder,
Sichelmond –
Mit der sanften Umarmung
Der Liebenden,
Den Schatten berühmter Zeiten
Die modernden Felsen rings;
So bläulich erstrahlt es
Gegen die Stadt hin,
Wo kalt und böse
Ein verwesend Geschlecht wohnt,
Der weissen Enkel
Dunkle Zukunft bereitet.
Ihr mondverschlungnen Schatten
Aufseufzend im leeren Kristall
Des Bergsees.

Evening

With dead figures of heroes
The moon is filling
The silent forests
O sickle-moon!
And the mouldering rocks all round
With the soft embraces
Of lovers,
The phantoms of famous ages;
This blue light shines
Towards the city
Where a decaying race
Lives coldly and evilly,
Preparing the dark future
Of their white descendants.
O moon-wrapped shadows
Sighing in the empty crystal
Of the mountain lake.

[D.L.]

Die Nacht

Dich sing ich wilde Zerklüftung,
Im Nachtsturm
Aufgetürmtes Gebirge;
Ihr grauen Türme
Überfliessend von höllischen Fratzen,
Feurigem Getier,
Rauhen Farnen, Fichten,
Kristallnen Blumen.
Unendliche Qual,
Dass du Gott erjagtest
Sanfter Geist,
Aufseufzend im Wassersturz.
In wogenden Föhren.

Golden lodern die Feuer
Der Völker rings.
Über schwärzliche Klippen
Stürzt todestrunken
Die erglühende Windsbraut,
Die blaue Woge
Des Gletschers
Und es dröhnt
Gewaltig die Glocke im Tal:
Flammen, Flüche
Und die dunklen
Spiele der Wollust,
Stürmt den Himmel
Ein versteinertes Haupt.

Night

You, wild fissure, I sing
In the night's storm
Upon towering mountains;
You – grey tower dungeons
Overflowing with hellish grimaces,
Fiery animals, rough
Ferns, spruce,
Crystal flowers.
Interminable pain
So that you hunt God
Gentle spirit,
Deeply sighing in the waterfall,
In swaying Scotch fir.

Golden, the fire flares up
About the nations.
Over blackish cliffs, dead
Drunk, crashes
The luminous tornado,
The blue comber of
The glacier
And powerfully
Tolls the bell in the valley:
Flames, curses
And the dark
Play of lust –
A petrified head
Storms heaven.

[R.G.]

Die Schwermut

Gewaltig bist du dunkler Mund
Im Innern, aus Herbstgewölk
Geformte Gestalt,
Goldner Abendstille;
Ein grünlich dämmernder Bergstrom
In zerbrochner Föhren
Schattenbezirk;
Ein Dorf,
Das fromm in braunen Bildern abstirbt.

Da springen die schwarzen Pferde
Auf nebliger Weide.
Ihr Soldaten!
Vom Hügel, wo sterbend die Sonne rollt,
Stürzt das lachende Blut –
Unter Eichen
Sprachlos! O grollende Schwermut
Des Heers; ein strahlender Helm
Sank klirrend von purpurner Stirne.

Herbstesnacht so kühle kommt,
Erglänzt mit Sternen
Über zerbrochenem Männergebein
Die stille Mönchin.

Melancholy

Dark mouth, you are inwardly
Powerful, form
Moulded by autumn clouds,
Golden evening stillness;
A green
Darkening mountain torrent in
Shattered Scotch pine shadows;
A village
That fades, peaceful in sepia prints.

Then gallop the black stallions
In misty fields.
Soldiers! From the hill
Where the sun rolls, dying,
Plunges the smiling blood –
Below oaks,
Voiceless! O rancorous melancholy
Of the army; a luminous helmet
Sank clanking from a purple forehead.

Autumn night, so cool, advances –
Sparkling with stars
Over shattered human bones:
The quiet moon-nun.

[R.G.]

Die Heimkehr

Die Kühle dunkler Jahre,
Schmerz und Hoffnung
Bewahrt zyklopisch Gestein,
Menschenleeres Gebirge,
Des Herbstes goldner Odem,
Abendwolke –
Reinheit!

Anschaut aus blauen Augen
Kristallne Kindheit;
Unter dunklen Fichten
Liebe, Hoffnung,
Da von feurigen Lidern
Tau ins starre Gras tropft –
Unaufhaltsam!

O! dort der goldene Steg
Zerbrechend im Schnee
Des Abgrunds!
Blaue Kühle
Odmet das nächtige Tal,
Glaube, Hoffnung!
Gegrüsst du einsamer Friedhof!

Homecoming

The dark years' coolness,
Pain and hope
Confirmed by Cyclopean stone,
Abandoned mountains, gold
Breath of fall,
Evening clouds –
Clarity!

Crystalline childhood gazes
From blue eyes;
Below dark spruce –
Love, hope;
So that, out of fiery eyelids,
Dew drips into stiff grass
Uncheckably!

Look! the golden footbridge
Shattering into the snow
Of the abyss!
The night valley
Breathes blue coolness –
Faith, hope!
Lonely churchyard, greetings.

[R.G.]

Im Osten

Den wilden Orgeln des Wintersturms
Gleicht des Volkes finstrer Zorn,
Die purpurne Woge der Schlacht,
Entlaubter Sterne.

Mit zerbrochnen Brauen, silbernen Armen
Winkt sterbenden Soldaten die Nacht.
Im Schatten der herbstlichen Esche
Seufzen die Geister der Erschlagenen.

Dornige Wildnis umgürtet die Stadt.
Von blutenden Stufen jagt der Mond
Die erschrockenen Frauen.
Wilde Wölfe brachen durchs Tor.

Eastern Front

The wrath of the people is dark,
Like the wild organ notes of winter storm,
The battle's crimson wave, a naked
Forest of stars.

With ravaged brows, with silver arms
To dying soldiers night comes beckoning.
In the shade of the autumn ash
Ghosts of the fallen are sighing.

Thorny wilderness girdles the town about.
From bloody doorsteps the moon
Chases terrified women.
Wild wolves have poured through the gates.

[C.M.]

Klage

Schlaf und Tod, die düstern Adler
Umrauschen nachtlang dieses Haupt:
Des Menschen goldnes Bildnis
Verschlänge die eisige Woge
Der Ewigkeit. An schaurigen Riffen
Zerschellt der purpurne Leib.
Und es klagt die dunkle Stimme
Über dem Meer.
Schwester stürmischer Schwermut
Sieh, ein ängstlicher Kahn versinkt
Unter Sternen,
Dem schweigenden Antlitz der Nacht.

Lament

Sleep and death, the dark eagles
Around this head swoop all night long:
Eternity's icy wave
Would swallow the golden image
Of man; against horrible reefs
His purple body is shattered.
And the dark voice laments
Over the sea.
Sister of stormy sadness,
Look, a timorous boat goes down
Under stars,
The silent face of the night.

[M.H.]

Grodek

Am Abend tönen die herbstlichen Wälder
Von tödlichen Waffen, die goldnen Ebenen
Und blauen Seen, darüber die Sonne
Düstrer hinrollt; umfängt die Nacht
Sterbende Krieger, die wilde Klage
Ihrer zerbrochenen Münder.
Doch stille sammelt im Weidengrund
Rotes Gewölk, darin ein zürnender Gott wohnt,
Das vergossne Blut sich, mondne Kühle;
Alle Strassen münden in schwarze Verwesung.
Unter goldnem Gezweig der Nacht und Sternen
Es schwankt der Schwester Schatten durch den
    schweigenden Hain,
Zu grüssen die Geister der Helden, die blutenden
    Häupter;
Und leise tönen im Rohr die dunklen Flöten des
    Herbstes.
O stolzere Trauer! ihr ehernen Altäre,
Die heisse Flamme des Geistes nährt heute ein ge-
    waltiger Schmerz,
Die ungebornen Enkel.

Grodek*

At nightfall the autumn woods cry out
With deadly weapons and the golden plains,
The deep blue lakes, above which more darkly
Rolls the sun; the night embraces
Dying warriors, the wild lament
Of their broken mouths.
But quietly there in the pastureland
Red clouds in which an angry god resides,
The shed blood gathers, lunar coolness.
All the roads lead to blackest carrion.
Under golden twigs of the night and stars
The sister's shade now sways through the silent copse
To greet the ghosts of the heroes, the bleeding heads;
And softly the dark flutes of autumn sound in the
    reeds.
O prouder grief! You brazen altars,
Today a great pain feeds the hot flame of the spirit,
The grandsons yet unborn.

[M.H.]

---

* A town in Galicia, Poland, where Trakl served as a chemist
with the Austrian army. A battle was fought there, after
which he was placed in charge of a large number of serious
casualties, whose sufferings he could not relieve; he tried to
shoot himself but was prevented. This was his last poem:
soon after writing it, he was sent to Cracow to be placed
under observation as a mental case. He died in a military
hospital there, from an overdose of drugs. (*Translator's note.*)

SELECTED BIBLIOGRAPHY

A list of the principal works of Georg Trakl with the dates
of their first appearance

GEDICHTE (Bücherei Der jüngste Tag, nos. 7, 8: Kurt
   Wolff, Leipzig, 1913)

SEBASTIAN IM TRAUM (Kurt Wolff, Leipzig, 1915)

DIE DICHTUNGEN, edited by K. Röck (Kurt Wolff, Leip-
   zig, 1919)

DER HERBST DES EINSAMEN (Studenbücher, no. 1:
   Kurt Wolff, Munich, 1920)

DIE DICHTUNGEN, with a Preface by Ludwig von Ficker
   (Ullman, Zwickau, 1928)

DIE DICHTUNGEN, edited by Kurt Horwitz (Die Arche,
   Zurich, 1946)

OFFENBARUNG UND UNTERGANG. DIE PROSADICHTUNGEN
   (O. Müller, Salzburg, 1947)

NACHLASS UND BIOGRAPHIE. GEDICHTE, BRIEFE, BILDER,
   ESSAYS, edited by Wolfgang Schneditz (O. Müller,
   Salzburg, 1949)

GESAMMELTE WERKE, edited by Wolfgang Schneditz
   (O. Müller, Salzburg, 1949–51)

Among previous translations of Trakl into English:

AN ANTHOLOGY OF GERMAN POETRY, 1880–1940, edited
   by Jethro Bithell (Methuen, London, 1941)

DECLINE, translated by Michael Hamburger (The Latin
   Press, Guido Morris, St Ives, 1952)

THE PENGUIN BOOK OF GERMAN VERSE, edited by Leonard Forster (Penguin Books, Harmondsworth, 1957)

TWENTY POEMS BY GEORG TRAKL, translated by James Wright and Robert Bly (The Sixties Press, Madison, Minnesota, 1961)

MODERN GERMAN POETRY, 1910–1960, edited by Michael Hamburger and Christopher Middleton (MacGibbon & Kee, London, 1962)

THE AUTHOR

Georg Trakl was born on February 3rd, 1887, in Salzburg, Austria and trained as a chemist. From 1908 he had to spend two years in Vienna and his first mature poems date from the end of that period. He did a year of military service in 1910–11, after which a second sojourn in Vienna again proved highly productive. In August 1914, Trakl was drafted into the Austrian army as a reserve lieutenant-pharmacist, and less than three months later, on November 3rd, 1914, he died of an overdose of drugs in Cracow, Poland.